"1 box for Fan Fox!" said Kit Cat.

Fan Fox got a cot. Fan sat.

"1 box for Fan Fox!" said Kit Cat.

Fan Fox got a fig. Fan bit it.

"1 box for Fan Fox!" said Kit Cat.

Fan Fox got a . Fan hit it.

"1 box for Fan Fox!" said Kit Cat.

Fan Fox got a lamp. Fan lit it.

"1 box for Fan Fox!" said Kit Cat.

Fan Fox got a fan. Fan ran it.

"1 BIG box for Fan Fox!" said Kit Cat.

"Not an ox!" said Fan Fox.

Fan Fox got the ox box for

the cot,

the fig,

the ,

the lamp,

and the fan.

"An ox for Kit Cat!" said Fan Fox.

"And a lot in the box!"